Cotton Candy

An Early Reader Series

Book 2

Annie Brown and
Alpha Omega Staff

Illustrated by Samar Waterworth
and Alpha Omega Staff

Alpha Omega Publications
300 North McKemy Avenue
Chandler, Arizona 85226-2618

ALPHA
OMEGA
PUBLICATIONS INC.

Instant Words

1.	the	he	go	who
2.	a	I	see	an
3.	is	they	then	their
4.	you	one	us	she
5.	to	good	no	new
6.	and	me	him	said
7.	we	about	by	did
8.	that	had	was	boy
9.	in	if	come	three
10.	not	some	get	down
11.	for	up	or	work
12.	at	her	two	put
13.	with	do	man	were
14.	it	when	little	before
15.	on	so	has	just
16.	can	my	them	long
17.	will	very	how	here
18.	are	all	like	other

Instant Words

19.	of	would	our	old
20.	this	any	what	take
21.	your	been	know	cat
22.	as	out	make	again
23.	but	there	which	give
24.	be	from	much	after
25.	have	day	his	many
26.	sand	jump	Tammy	shoes
27.	sailboat			

The Red Ball

Jan has a ball.

It is big and red.

It is fun to catch.

Dan will call Jan.

Jan will let go of her ball.

The ball will go up, up, up.

Is it a ball?

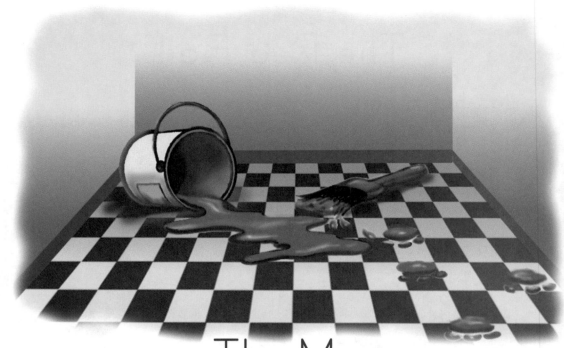

The Mess

What is this?
Who did it?
Who did this mess?
Dan did not do it.
He was in the back.
Kim did not do it.
She was at the job.
Who did it?

Fun!

Jan will have fun!
She will dig in the sand.
She will mix the sand.
She will pat the sand.
She will fix the sand.
Jan will have fun!

Pets

I have a dog and a cat.
The cat is black.
The dog is tan.
I run and run.
The pets run and run!
What fun it is to have a pet!

The Cowboy

Jim is a cowboy!
Jim will hop on his sawhorse, Buttercup.
Jim has a wish.
When Jim gets big,
Jim will get a job on a big ranch.
Then Jim will hop on Buttercup and go
up the hill.
Yip-Yip-Yip!

The Pup and the Box

A pup has a box.
It is a small box.
The box is shut.

The pup will tug at the box.
The lid will pop up.
The small man will jump up!

Pigs

Pigs will get wet in the mud.
The pigs will grab the cobs.
The pigs will slip in the mud.
The pigs will trip.
But, the pigs will grip
the cobs.

Fish, Fish, Fish

We will catch fish.
You will catch a big fish.
I will catch a big fish.
The sun will get hot.
It will not stop the fish.
It will not stop us.
What fun to fish, fish, fish!

Ann and the Fish

Dad and Ann will fish.

Ann will sit still.

A fish will grab the string.

Ann will jump.

Ann will hop and tug.

She will tug and tug.

Ann will catch a fish!

Glad Tammy

Tammy is glad.
She will clap.
She will jump.
She has shoes that fit!
Tammy will thank Mom and Dad.
Tammy will thank God.

I Talk To God

I talk to God.

I ask God to help us.

I ask God to help Mom.

I ask God to help Dad.

God will help us.

The Gift

Bill will get a gift for Beth.
Will he get a brown doll?
Will he get a sailboat?
Will he get a lot of things?
Bill will think and think.
Then, Bill will get a gift for Beth.

Three Missing Pups

BOOM!

Kaboom! went the thunder.

Jen and Freddie ran to the blue shed.

They hid behind a tall yellow can.

13

"Where are the three pups?" asked
Freddie.

"I do not see them," said Jen.

"We must find them fast," said Freddie
and Jen at the same time.

BOOM!

Kaboom! went the thunder.

The sky was getting black.

Jen and Freddie ran to the house.

"Have you seen our three pups?" Freddie
asked Mom.

"No, I have not", said Mom.

"We must find them fast," said Freddie
and Jen at the same time.

"Let's think about this," said Jen.

They went to all the rooms and called
their names.

The last room was Jen's.

Then, she heard a thumping sound.

She looked on her bed and saw three lumps.

"I think I found our three pups," she said.

BOOM! BOOM! KABOOOOOOOM! went the thunder.

In Mom came down the hall.

"Where did everyone go?" called Mom.

Then she looked in Jen's room and saw five lumps on the bed!

Clickety Clack

Clickety clack, Clickety clack
What goes down this railroad track?

It is gray and it is long.
It is fast and it is strong.

What goes down this railroad track?

Clickety clack, Clickety clack

It is big and it is black.
It goes there and then comes back.

What goes down this railroad track?

Clickety clack. Clickety clack.

The Twins Fix Lunch

The twins will fix lunch for the children.
It will be fun! It will be yummy!

Ed gets the ham and cheese.
He cuts them into small chunks.

Ted gets the apples and bananas.
He cuts them into small chunks, too.

Ed and Ted put the chunks on a big platter.
Ted calls the children.

The hungry children come running.
They see ham chunks, cheese chunks, apple
and banana chunks.

"How can we eat this kind of lunch?"
they ask.
"I know" says Ed.

Ed and Ted put their lunch chunks in little cups.

The children cheer. "Thank you Ted and Ed!"
"This lunch is fun. This lunch is yummy!"
"This lunch is chunky!"

The New Little Bug

Katy and Joey like to hunt for bugs.
They look in the tall grass.

They look in the cracks of the sidewalk.
"Bugs are everywhere," said Joey.
"We can find all kinds."

One day Katy saw a bug on a twig. "I have never seen a bug like this," said Katy. "It is so tiny. It is black and red with six very small legs. I like this bug", she said. "I can't wait to show my friend, Joey."

Katy picked the little bug up and put it in her hand. She took it over to Joey's and showed him. He liked it, too.

   "Let's get a book and find out what kind it is," he said.

Just then a small gust of wind
came along. Katy's bug was gone!

"I guess we'll just have to remember what
it looked like," said Katy.

"And don't forget," said Joey, "It can
fly, too!"

Betty the Bat

Betty the bat is an acrobat.

I watch her flap her wings.
Flip, flap it's like a dance.
She's up above my head.

Betty the bat is an acrobat.
I watch her twist and twirl.
She can fly up and she can
fly down.
There she goes round and round.

Betty the bat is an acrobat!

Black and White Keys

I sit and look at the black and white keys.
The long, long row of black and white
keys.

Tap! I push one down. "Plunk!"
It makes a sound.
Tap, tap! I push two down. "Plink, Plunk!"
They make a new sound.

Down go the keys.
Up come the keys.
Down, up, down, up.
I do this all day long.

I sit and look at the black and white keys.
The long, long row of black and white keys.
My fingers dance on the black and white keys.
"Plink, plunk, plink, plink, plunk."

They make a lovely sound.
They make a lovely song.

A Big Problem

"Hello, Mrs. Hippopotamus," said Mr. Crocodile.

"What is all this fuss?"

"Well, Mr. Crocodile," said Mrs.
Hippopotamus,
"I would like to take a bath. It really is
a must.
But as you can see my tub is a dud.
The water is gone.
There is nothing but mud."

"I wish I could help you,"
Mrs. Hippopotamus.

"I understand your
fuss.
But as you can
see, I am just a
crocodile
and mud
is fine with me."

Little Lamb

"Little Lamb, Little Lamb, where are you?" called the Shepherd.

"Baaaa, Baaaa," called Little Lamb, but the Shepherd couldn't hear her. She was too far away.

Little Lamb knew she shouldn't wander off to High Hill.

Little Lamb knew she should stay with the rest of the sheep inside the white fence. "There could be danger," she would hear the Shepherd say.

But Little Lamb didn't listen. She was tired of the same old grassy field.

High Hill couldn't be that bad! So Little Lamb wandered off to High Hill.

Now it was night and Little Lamb was lost and afraid. She was sorry she didn't obey the Shepherd.

"Baaaa, Baaaaa," she called louder and louder.

The Shepherd watched by the fence all night, but he did not see her.

"I will not rest until I find her," he said. He kept calling Little Lamb by name.

Then, just before the sun came up, the Shepherd heard, "Baaaaa, Baaaaa." It was Little Lamb!

He called back to her until she found her way to the white fence.

He was so glad to see her he gave her a big hug.

Little Lamb knew the Shepherd loved her so much.

She never wanted to wander away from him again.

Cotton Candy

"It's here! It's here! The circus is here!" the children shouted. They were excited.

Alex went to the circus last summer and couldn't wait to see it again. The best part, he said, was the cotton candy!

Finally it was the big day. Alex's family was going to the circus. Alex knew he would see clowns and funny animal tricks, but most of all he wanted some fluffy, pink and blue cotton candy.

When Alex and his family got there, they went inside the big tent. It was filled with people! They saw acrobats swinging in the air and dogs that could dance.

Alex liked the acts, but he couldn't stop thinking about cotton candy.

Next, Alex and his sister got a balloon. Alex's balloon was blue. His sister's was

pink. He liked his balloon, but he couldn't stop thinking about cotton candy.

"Can we get a snack?" he asked his mom and dad.

"Sure," they said. "What would you like?"

Alex didn't even have to think about it. "Cotton candy!" he shouted.

Then he saw the candy shop. They must have cotton candy, he thought. He walked in a circle around the shop, once, then twice. Finally, after three times a nice man came out and asked if he could help him. "Yes, yes!" Alex said. "I would like pink and blue cotton candy."

"That will be ten cents," said the man.

Alex dug into his pocket and pulled out five pennies and one nickel. "I have just enough," he said. "Here is ten cents."

Now Alex didn't have to think about cotton candy for the rest of the day. Smack, smack!
went his pink and blue lips
with a big smile.

The Last Trick

"No more chances for you!" yelled the boys as they ran away.

Jack's brothers were mad that he had tricked them again. Jack tossed mud balls at them as they ran away. He laughed and laughed. This was the second time he had called for help.

His brothers, Jed and Jim, had come running fast. Jack was smaller than them, and it was their job to look after him.

Later that same day, Jack climbed the tall ladder to get to the highest branch on the big elm tree. He sat there for awhile watching the others play. When it was time to get down, the ladder wobbled and Jack was afraid. He didn't know how to get down. He called for help, but the boys just walked away.

Jack was sad that no one wanted to help him. He had played too many tricks on them. He knew they didn't trust him.

After sitting on the branch a long time, Jack's Uncle Mick asked him if he wanted help getting down. "Yes," said Jack. "I'm stuck on this branch and it is not a trick."

"I will help you then," said Uncle Mick.

"Thank you, Uncle Mick," said Jack, giving him a big hug. "I will not play those kinds of tricks again."

The Lemonade Stand

Stella and Stan have a plan for the hot summer days. They ran inside to talk to Mom.

"We have a plan for these hot summer days," said Stan. "We want to make a lemonade stand."

"That's great," replied Mom. "Make a list of the things you need. Look around the house so you won't need to spend a lot of money."

So Stella and Stan made a list of what they would need. They looked around the house.

First, they got a jug for the lemonade.

"We'll need to scrub it," said Stella.

Then, they got a big, brown box to stand in.

"We'll need to cut a hole for a window," said Stan.

Next, they got some yellow, blue and green cups.

"All we need now is the lemonade," said Stella.

"We can buy it at the store," said Stan.

"Mom was right. We didn't have to spend a lot of money!" shouted Stella.

Stella and Stan were ready. They had everything they needed, but no one was coming to buy lemonade.

"What did we forget?" asked Stella.

"I know," said Stan.

He ran to get paper and crayons. He wrote something on the paper. Then Stan stuck the paper on the front of the box.

"Now we can sell lemonade", he said. "Look! Here comes our first customer!"

Stuck Again

"Oh, no!" cried Skippy the Squid. "I can't be stuck again."

Before lunch he had gotten stuck in an old rock. After that he got stuck in a sunken ship. Now he was stuck in the middle of a thick clump of seaweed.

"Another day of bad luck," he thought. "Good thing I have a friend like Oscar."

But Oscar wasn't nearby this time.

As others passed by, Skippy called to them for help.

"Will you help me get out of this sea-weed?" he asked Tim Tuna.

"No, I can't. I have someplace else to go," answered Tim.

"Can you get me out of these twisted plants?" he asked Sherry Shark.

"Oh, I'm much too busy," she replied.

Then Skippy saw his good friend, Oscar.
He was swinging his fish friends around

on his eight, strong arms just like a merry-go-round. Swish and swirl, around they all went.

"What fun that would be," thought Skippy, "but not for me. I'm stuck in the seaweed."

"Don't lose hope," he heard someone say softly.

Just then, Oscar blasted through the thick plants with his eight, strong arms and got Skippy out.

"Thank you, Oscar! You're the best," said Skippy.

"I'm glad I saw you, Skippy. Now you can play, too," said Oscar.

So Skippy grabbed on to one of Oscar's arms. His fish friends grabbed the others.

"Here we go!" Oscar swirled them around and around.

It was great fun, but Skippy couldn't stop thinking about those soft words that told him to not to lose hope.

As they turned around one more time, he saw a little seahorse slip through the twisted seaweed. The little seahorse smiled at him and then slipped away.